2015
THE **JAMES BACKHOUSE** LECTURE

This we can do

Quaker faith in action through the Alternatives to Violence Project

SALLY HERZFELD AND ALTERNATIVES TO VIOLENCE PROJECT MEMBERS

THE **JAMES BACKHOUSE** LECTURES

The lectures were instituted by Australia Yearly
Meeting of the Religious Society of Friends
(Quakers) on its establishment in 1964.

They are named after James Backhouse who, with his
companion, George Washington Walker, visited Australia
from 1832 to 1838. They travelled widely, but spent most
of their time in Tasmania. It was through their visit that
Quaker Meetings were first established in Australia.

Coming to Australia under a concern for the conditions of
convicts, the two men had access to people with authority
in the young colonies, and with influence in Britain, both in
Parliament and in the social reform movement. In meticulous
reports and personal letters, they made practical suggestions
and urged legislative action on penal reform, on the rum
trade, and on land rights and the treatment of Aborigines.

James Backhouse was a general naturalist and a botanist. He
made careful observations and published full accounts of what
he saw, in addition to encouraging Friends in the colonies and
following the deep concern that had brought him to Australia.

Australian Friends hope that this series of Lectures will bring fresh
insights into the Truth, and speak to the needs and aspirations
of Australian Quakerism. The present lecture was delivered at
Queen's College, the University of Melbourne, on 5 January 2015.

Julian Robertson
Presiding Clerk
Australia Yearly Meeting

ISBN 978-0-9923857-2-9

Produced by Australia Yearly Meeting of the Religious Society of
Friends (Quakers) in Australia Incorporated
Download copies from www.quakers.org.au
or order from http://ipoz.biz/Store/orders.htm

Quakers
AUSTRALIA

Front cover: Sally Herzfeld with
grandchildren and great-grandchildren.
Photo: John Herzfeld

Contents

Acknowledgments

Participants of the Regional Gathering in Australia in January 2014 for the initial brainstorming of ideas for the lecture.

Elizabeth Kwan for her patience, continual encouragement and expert advice.

My husband, Tom, for his support and tolerance of papers everywhere

My son, John, for his happily given IT assistance

AVP colleagues in Australia and other countries, who have been generous with information.

The AYM Backhouse Lecture Committee for its commitment to the publication and delivery of this lecture.

About the author

Alison, the second of five children of Elsie and Cyril Gare, grew up in the hills near Perth in the village of Darlington. Once staunch Anglicans, Cyril and Elsie became Friends in the mid-1940s and their children gradually became members with them. Alison's name changed to Al, then Ali and finally, Sally.

With parents supporting the United Nations, Aboriginal welfare and several Society of Friends' projects, it is no wonder that Sally became involved in some of these, too. But she was also a keen Girl Guide, who earned the Queen's Guide award and later was a Guide leader of companies in four different places.

She qualified as a teacher of Early Childhood, but has taught all grades since then. Her first appointment was for two wonderful years at the Forrest River Mission (now Umbulgurri) in the far north of Western Australia. Here she gratefully received the gift of a primus stove from the Friends Service Council (FSC). Later, while teaching back near Perth, she was involved with her parents at the Allawah Grove Aboriginal Settlement. Here the FSC had a project to help improve the people's living standards.

Her next appointment in September 1959 was to start a school in Port Hedland for Aboriginal children who hadn't attended school before and couldn't speak English. During the following two and a third years she was again welcomed into an Aboriginal community and learned to love these people and plenty about their culture before alcohol and drugs intervened.

Marrying Tom Herzfeld in 1962, Sally had to follow the rule of the day and leave teaching to be a good wife and mother. Tom was a civil engineer with the Water Supply. While travelling the state they had three children, John, Wendy and Andrew before settling back into Darlington in 1969.

Three years later she and Tom bought a small private school in Darlington. The newly-formed school council gradually bought the block and classroom from them, with Sally as principal for ten years. The primary school developed and in 1988 she became the coordinator of a new high school on a different campus. Her involvement with Helena College still continues.

Sally's AVP journey started in 2002 when she trained in Acacia Prison for men, to become a facilitator. She considers herself very lucky since then to have been able to facilitate workshops in schools, prisons and with different community groups around Australia and in other countries.

Although family time with the three children, nine grandchildren and four great grandchildren takes priority, Sally is chair of the board of a women's refuge, joins refugee women for cooking and handcraft activities, and is treasurer of AVP WA. She is grateful for her very full and interesting life.

Prologue

The changing use of the Backhouse Lecture

One of the joys of serving on the Backhouse Lecture Committee is seeing the variety of people and the issues they care about brought to the Committee for consideration, and recommending one of them as the nominated lecturer. We learn something of their background, their work, and why this has attracted the attention of those nominating their names. Once a recommendation is made, the Committee begins to accompany the lecturers on their journey reading drafts, giving comments and assisting when requested. It is a journey of about two years.

Since the first Backhouse Lecture in 1964, the committee has usually recommended one name, though on five occasions, when there were two names, reflecting joint involvement in a specific concern, a joint lecture was presented. However, in 2010 there were many Backhouse Lecturers as Young Friends wrote and presented their journey in finding their voice among Australian Quakers. The published booklet listed fifty-four names as authors, and in presentation and its recording, many of those named declared that they were the Backhouse Lecturer. Most recently, Tracy Bourne, urging us to bring children into the centre of Quaker life and worship, drew her husband and children into the lecture as an example of how that could be done.

In February 2013 the committee hoped Sally Herzfeld would be the 2015 lecturer because of her deep knowledge of, and experience with the Alternatives to Violence Project (AVP) in Australia and overseas. She would speak powerfully to the peace testimony at a time when Australians would be commemorating the impact of World War 1 on Australia. Sally was clear in her response that, given the strong tradition of team work in AVP, she wished to include the voices and contributions of others in writing and speaking about the transforming effect AVP has had on many lives. The committee welcomes this development.

Elizabeth Kwan

Coordinator, AVP Darwin

Member, Backhouse Lecture Committee since 2011

1. Quakers and the Alternatives to Violence Project

'There is good in everyone.'

'Look for and affirm the good in self and others.'

'We're all teachers and all learners.'

Friends, do these statements sound familiar?

Can you imagine that George Fox would have thought this way?

We all have a power for good within us. There is no need for intermediaries.

Founding philosophy

Quakers have held one very clear philosophy since George Fox's time: that there is 'That of God within everyone'. This belief can be considered as the foundation of many Quaker commitments, such as pacifism or the continual striving for social justice, and the search for nonviolent methods to work things out while still maintaining integrity and respect for self.

Is it any wonder that Quakers had a big influence on the beginning of the Alternatives to Violence Project (AVP)? The statements above form part of AVP's philosophy and guidelines.

Quakers' Peace Testimony reflects a 'vision of the world transformed by Christ who lives in the hearts of all'. Quakers tried

… to make the vision real by putting emphasis on Christian practice rather than primarily on any particular dogma or ideological system. Theirs was a spontaneous and practical religion. They recognised the realities of evil and conflict, but it was contrary to the spirit of Christ to use war and violence as means to deal with them.[1]

Quakers and prison work

Quakers from the early years were closely involved in working with prisoners. Elizabeth Fry's example in the nineteenth century is well known, and there have been many other Quakers since then. For Elizabeth, when she wrote in 1827 about her work,

Much depends on the spirit in which the visitor enters upon her work. It must be in the spirit, not of judgement, but of mercy. She must not say in her heart, I am more holy than thou, but must rather keep in perpetual remembrance that 'all have sinned and come short of the Glory of God'.[2]

The Alternatives to Violence Project started in a New York prison in 1975, and the humility Elizabeth wrote about has marked the manner of most AVP facilitators since then, as they enter prisons to conduct a workshop.

Since George Fox's time, many Quakers were imprisoned for their beliefs and supported by Quaker prison ministers and visitors. Quaker prison ministers in Britain, recognised like other religious prison chaplains, used to conduct Meetings for Worship within prisons. Hence Quakers (whether as inmates or outmates), and prisons have been closely linked for centuries. They have committed civil disobedience in defending human rights, protesting against the government of the day, and promoting civil rights and environmental concerns. Jo Vallentine, a well-known Australian activist, uses the positive descriptor of 'Holy Obedience'.

Jo is Western Australia's own present-day Quaker activist. She recalled her experiences in the Alice Springs jail, after committing Holy Obedience. Although she knew a little of what prison would be like, she found the actual experience of being a prisoner pretty shattering and dehumanising. She meditated a lot, but was still 'really angry that our government was allowing Australian soil to be used to further the nuclear war fighting plans of another nation'.[3]

However, as she explained in 1991, she thought about

... the other message that was Gandhi's very strong message, which is the transforming power of love. And that has to come through in a public sense, because if you're involved in working for peace, there's no point in looking really angry about it, even though the anger might be part of your motivating force. But you really do need also to think about why other people have a very different view from yours. You have to try to understand it and, really, think very much as you do with a child: 'I don't like your behaviour, but I can still love your being'. I constantly remind myself that our call is to passion and action – you see, the two things are close together, but they've got to be underpinned by love. Otherwise, you're really not making any sense at all. Unless that spiritual and loving element is there, what are you doing it for?

Jo Vallentine was the main driving force behind getting AVP started in Western Australia.

The beginnings of AVP

AVP began in the Green Haven Maximum Security prison in New York in 1975. A group of inmates who were mainly of African descent, calling themselves the 'Think Tank', was concerned about the violence between youth gangs and the way some young prisoners were coming in and out of jail several times. Steve Angell, as a Quaker visitor and professional social worker, later reported that the 'Think Tank' inmates were not having much success with the scare tactics they were using: 'You keep going the way you are and you'll end up where we are. This is what prison is like' and so forth.[4]

The first workshop devised by the prison inmates drew on the help and experience of several organisations, programs and individuals, including the Movement for a New Society and the Children's Creative Response to Conflict Program.[5] However, the most important of these were two groups: the Quakers, who had trained the marshals keeping the demonstrations against the Vietnam War peaceful; and those committed to the peaceful struggle for civil rights. Steve Angell explained:

> ... because we had a Quaker worship group there in the prison they knew that during the Vietnam War years they'd heard that we had trained thousands of marshals to go into demonstrations and help keep them nonviolent. So they said, 'Could you come and teach us something about how to teach nonviolence?' So the first workshop was born at Green Haven at the request of inmates.

Quakers had begun nonviolent training in 1960 with the New York Yearly Meeting

Peace Action Program. Its organisation was the Quaker Project of Community Conflict, headed by Lee Stern.[6] A founding director was Lawrence (Larry) Apsey, who after World War II had become a pacifist and a Quaker, influenced by the thinking of Mahatma Gandhi. Invited to Green Haven prison with Stern in 1975, Apsey aimed to help youth break out of their psychology of total violence and benefit both the youth and the community to which they would return.[7]

Also influential during this time was Bernard LaFayette, a Baptist minister who devoted his life to nonviolence and civil rights. He was one of the Freedom Riders of the anti-segregation movement who travelled through the South in the 1960s and became famous in Jackson, Mississippi. He has continued to lead nonviolence training and activities to this day. Faye (Honey) Knopps, a Quaker prison reform advocate, involved LaFayette in devising a nonviolence workshop for inmates after riots broke out in the prison at El Remo, Oklahoma. They were able to include both sides of a riot and the prison guards in the same workshop. More riots occurred in other prisons and Apsey contacted Knopps because he wanted the help of skilled people to enable him to bring nonviolent methods into New York prisons. Knopps referred Apsey to LaFayette, and that is how he came to be on the first team to facilitate the very successful workshop in Green Haven in 1975.[8]

Apsey, also a retired attorney, went on in 1979 to form a corporation of the Quaker Project of Community Conflict and invited Angell to become a member of the Board of Directors. Angell believed that it was Apsey's effort 'that led to the expansion of the nonviolence training program in 1980 [when it] was officially launched as the Alternatives to Violence Project.' By 1981, Angell noted, the program had trained 1900 men and women in 19 prisons in New York and New Jersey, with 300 going on to the Advanced level and 120 becoming facilitators.

The program that was first developed began with sessions designed to build self-worth within each participant and community within the group. It concluded with strength-building discussions of twelve guidelines for the use of a power which can transform people and situations. Apsey described the nonviolence about which he spoke as 'being very firm and sometimes very aggressive in a nonviolent way'. Material was also taken from programs such as the Movement for a New Society and the Children's Creative Response to Conflict Program. LaFayette, who was Martin Luther King's co-ordinator of training, commented on the importance of role play, which was 'crucial to achieving nonviolent responses to violent outbursts that irate folks holding white supremacist views focused on civil rights protesters at lunch counters and on buses throughout the South'. He explained:

In our trainings we first strove to develop a grounding sense of the Blessed Community, one that includes overt racists and white supremacists. Then we had trainees take on the role of enraged people with racist views, even go so far as to strike the protesters, while the protesters tried to maintain an attitude of love and goodwill toward their attackers. This worked very well so that there were few inflammatory reactions when protesters experienced actual racial violence directed at them personally. Role playing was one of the facilitation skills I was quite familiar with. Perhaps my contributions helped to establish it as part of the AVP workshop experiences.[9]

Australian Quakers also used role plays in the 1970s in training for peaceful protesting during the Vietnam Moratorium marches. My Dad, Cyril Gare, led several Vietnam Moratorium marches in Perth, Western Australia, and I know he did some training to make sure that the marches would be as peaceful as possible. One day after coming home from a training session, he upset Mum by saying that he had been 'tickled all over'! I imagine that this was some kind of trust building exercise within the group or it might have been to practise resisting if someone tried to break up a human barricade of people with linked arms. We do not do this one in AVP!!

Other philosophies that I've heard or read about which we DO practice include:

- We will not use or return violence, physical or verbal, towards any person or property.
- We will not bring, or protest under the influence of, alcohol or illicit drugs.
- We will use a consensus decision making process to reach agreement within our group/s.

Dad, when running a training weekend, stirred up the participants by telling them that men and women had to sleep in different dormitories. Some were married couples and they were quite angry about this dictatorial decision making. He let them rant and rage for a while and then, after dinner, shocked them all by calmly saying, 'That was your first test!' The rest of the weekend was mainly role plays about possible violent situations that could arise during protests.

In AVP we use role plays to demonstrate and practise strategies and help participants gain confidence. They experience empathy when acting the role of someone who might have been their opposite in a conflict, and according to one inmate participant, 'We get to see what people behaving badly look like!' He had just watched a role play and

5

asked, 'Do we really look like that when we're drunk on the train??!'

In Melbourne, Frances Newell devised a program from her Quaker background and what she had read about Gandhi. Role playing was involved and I also understand that Quakers gave support and supplied a venue for gatherings at Melbourne Friends House, Orrong Road. They assisted a considerable number of conscientious objectors who were being pursued by police.

AVP development beyond the United States of America

Steve Angell later reflected that he had wondered how this program could ever work in a prison and did not know then that he would become so involved. He did not consider himself to be a violent person in need of that sort of training. After becoming a member of the board of directors and doing his first workshop, like many of us since then, he found out things about himself that he did not know before. In spite of his professional work, he realised that he wasn't really as in touch with his own feelings as he should be, to conduct even his own personal relationships in a better way. In 2006 at an AVP gathering in South Africa Steve told us that the program was called a long name until one day a prison officer met the team as they were leaving the workshop and asked how their alternatives to violence meeting went. That team thought that would be a very simple and descriptive name for their workshops so the Alternatives to Violence Project became the official name.

For some years the focus was on prisons and the major effort was to help people reduce the level of violence in the prison environment, to survive it and at the same time to deal with the violence in their own lives. Waiting lists grew in the prison and it wasn't long before it was realised that there was just as much violence in society and people began to request this same type of training. So AVP spread to communities and schools. The first official community workshop was held in Owega, New York at the instigation of two local probation officers. They wanted to help probationers cope with the problems that led to their delinquency, but also to create understanding of those problems within communities. The participants of workshops were a mixture of people who had been in trouble with the law and those who had not. As in all workshops now, community was built within this mixed group.

Angell, as a main team member, later took AVP to many parts of the world. I met him at an AVP International Gathering near Johannesburg in South Africa. With him, he had a tall Afro-American man, Robert Martin, who had travelled to many

6

places helping facilitate workshops with Steve. Robert told us about his initiation into AVP. He had had an unfortunate childhood, been a street kid and done all sorts of bad stuff. During his second time in prison, he thought he would try this program, so he went into the room with the other guys. He was lounging around waiting, feeling a bit cynical that anything would work for him, when in walked this group of Quakers, men with their baggy shorts and pink knees. 'Oh my God!' he thought. 'What am I doing here?' He misbehaved during the workshop and was really disruptive. At the end of the day, as he was leaving and deciding not to return the next day, this short man, Larry Apsey followed him out and said something like, 'From the few contributions you have made, I understand that you have had a hard life. What's happening for you now?' They talked for a while and the tall man said that he went back to his cell, took down the girlie pictures he had and replaced them with the handout about conflict resolution that he had received. He finished that workshop and the next two levels, then after release from prison, he joined Steve and facilitated with him in many different places around the world. Waiting lists grew in many prisons in the US then to communities, schools and prisons in other parts of the world.

Steve Angell and Robert Martin at the International Gathering in S. Africa 2006. Photo: Sally Herzfeld.

2. Alternatives to Violence Project around the world

Today independent groups of volunteers, linked by AVP International, are holding AVP workshops in about 60 countries around the world. [10]

Map from AVP International Website

Visiting Facilitators

To give an adequate history of how these groups emerged is not possible in this lecture. In general the focus of AVP groups has been organising workshops and training enough volunteers to present them. Very often these volunteers have full-time paid jobs and other commitments. Researching and writing a documented history of a group has been unthinkable in the face of these pressures. Knowing a few facts about the first workshop in a New York prison in 1975 seemed enough. Only in recent times are people in the US beginning to write histories of the AVP movement there. The search for material for this lecture has prompted an interest in the histories of the different Australian groups.

However, it is possible to sketch a rough outline of the movement of AVP across the world. Between 1975 and 1988, it spread rapidly in the states of USA. Clearly Steve Angell, the US Quaker from the early years of the American workshops, was one of the most dedicated carriers of the AVP message. From 1989 onwards, Quakers made a more concerted effort to take the message of nonviolence into parts of the world most affected by conflict. Steve trained facilitators everywhere he went so that while AVP continued strongly, mainly in prisons in USA, he was able to involve other facilitators to go to other countries with him or in separate teams.

From 1989 to 1994, it spread North to Canada and Alaska, then South to Central America, East to England, South East to New Zealand and Australia, then to Israel, Russia, Germany and Croatia. AVP in South Africa started in 1995 and in India, the first workshop was held under a Banyan tree in 1996. The next countries to experience AVP between 2001 and 2005 included some in Central and North Africa, then off we went in 2007 and 2008 to Palestine, Israel and Nepal. Between then and 2014 new groups have started in Indonesia, and workshops have been held in Ukraine, Papua New Guinea, the Philippines and Afghanistan.[11]

This historical time line is still evolving but for a more comprehensive list of where and by whom AVP was started in countries, please see the appendix.

Friends Peace Teams Initiatives

Perhaps the most interesting development in extending AVP workshops around the world has been the creation of the Friends Peace Teams network by Friends from several Yearly Meetings in the US in 1993.[12] Concerned about the genocide in Bosnia, they shared their knowledge of world conflicts and aimed to raise funds to enable volunteers to join peace teams in troubled communities. Every Friends Meeting House or Church would become a centre for peace-making. This work formed 'initiatives' to offer opportunities for communities in conflict to create human and material resources to assist them to build peace. The initial Coordinating Committee evolved into a Council to coordinate its projects around the world and represent the supporting US Yearly Meetings. Since 2013 the Council has included a representative of Australia Yearly Meeting.

The **African Great Lakes Initiative (AGLI)** was the first to become active with a tour of Quaker communities in **Kenya, Burundi, Uganda, Rwanda** and

Tanzania in 1999 by Friends from the USA, UK, Canada, and South Africa. The goal was to establish personal relationships with people in that very violent region and to learn about and support Friends' initiatives for building local peace.

The outcome was AGLI, based in Kenya, and coordinated by David Zarembka, who led the original delegation. It works on peace building activities in Burundi, Congo, Kenya, Rwanda and Uganda with its many partners in those countries and beyond. AVP workshops are a key tool, helping many people learn to manage their violent feelings. In Kenya, AVP has been used in many ways including in the large refugee camps near the Somali border. It has also been a key tool for an AGLI partner, the Kenya Friends Church Peace Team, which works to reconcile communities torn apart by the post-election violence in 2008. In Rwanda, AVP was used to train the judges working in the gacaca (community) courts in the aftermath of the genocide. There are many other examples in all five countries, and there is a large cohort of trained AVP facilitators.[13]

Friends used a combination of locally devised techniques combined with other programs as well as AVP. David Zarembka, a Baltimore Friend, has been the main energiser of AGLI and is its coordinator.

Peacebuilding en Las Americas (PLA) is the second initiative, evolved in 2002 with a visit to Columbia by four USA Friends, who were AVP facilitators, fluent in Spanish and had lived in Latin America.[14] Named the Latin America-Caribbean Initiative of Friends Peace Teams, it became Peacebuilding enLas Americas in 2010. Supported by Friends from all over USA and abroad, PLA works with communities in **Nicaragua, Honduras, El Salvador, Guatemala, Colombia** and **Bolivia.** The work there makes extensive use of AVP methods to reduce violence among individuals and groups. Val Liveoak has been the principal energiser of PLA and continues to serve as coordinator.

FPT – Asia West Pacific (AWP) is the most recent initiative. It developed after the 2004 tsunami devastated the province of **Aceh, Indonesia.** Working with Peace Brigade International from 1999 to 2004, a travelling Quaker, Nadine Hoover, supported by AVP-NY, established relationships with the Acehnese people isolated by thirty years of war. Alfred Friends Meeting (NY) supported her travel to Indonesia to help tsunami and war survivors in Aceh and **North Sumatra.** People in Aceh asked, 'Why do people care so much about tsunami victims? We were only hit one day. The war hits day after day after day. Why don't they care about war victims?'[15]

The work led by Nadine in the early years focused entirely on enabling communities to live peacefully in civil war stricken provinces of Indonesia. In 2007 it became Friends Peace Teams Indonesia Initiative, part of Asia West Pacific Friends Peace Teams since 2012. Most recently in Indonesia, FPT, together with Amnesty International and the Norwegian Embassy, helped ensure the security of thousands of refugees in Baruk Induk, North Sumatra, against the power of logging and palm oil interests. A closed and violent community has been transformed. Nadine's work has used AVP a great deal and has now developed an Indonesian community trauma healing methodology.

Since its origin in Indonesia, FPT AWP has grown to work in Palestine/Gaza, Israel, Nepal, Aceh, Afghanistan, Sumatra, Java and the Philippines and it is initiating relationships with First Nation leaders in Australia. AVP workshops are being held in these places.

Other Initiatives supported by Australian AVP Facilitators

Nepal AVP grew out of a chance meeting in 2007 on the steps of a cathedral in Geneva, between an Australian facilitator Aletia Dundas and Subhash Kattel, a young man from Kathmandu with a passion for peace and justice in his war-torn country. In 2008, with funding provided by team members, individuals in USA and the Australian Quaker Peace and Justice Fund, an Australian team consisting of Aletia, Katherine and Malcolm Smith and John Michaelis joined with locals Subhash Kattel and Ken Woods to run about ten workshops and train about 25 facilitators. The work continued to grow with about 100 workshops primarily around the capital in the valley of Kathmandu.

Towards the end of 2012, Friends Peace Teams began to support the development of AVP in Nepal. John Michaelis, who is a Quaker, an AVP facilitator, and Friends Peace Teams member, with links to both US and Australia, reported in May 2014:

A Training for Facilitators was held so that these people could run workshops in the refugee camps near Damak. Facilitators lived in the camps and ran more than 20 workshops in two months. During the following year two workshops [one on trauma, the other on discernment] were held in the capital and the first Basic workshop was run by a local AVP team in Pokhara – an eight-hour bus drive away.

In December 2013 a visiting group of facilitators ran a Trauma workshop in Kathmandu and this was possibly the first ever such workshop with participants who were victims of human trafficking. Next they ran two Basic workshops that included staff from the charity called 'Children Nepal'. This is a charity with a major concern for the beatings and other painful physical punishment meted out even to young children in the schools there.

In conjunction with 'Children Nepal' a small team returned in April and May 2014 to run workshops in remote villages. Conditions were very basic and rough and it is amazing that the team was able to stay to help teachers in the district find nonviolent ways to teach while still maintaining order. The deep concern of these teachers was that children must be able to grow up free from systemic and institutionalised physical violence. We are proud that AVP can help with this.

The next adventure was to run a workshop at a university in Surkhet in the mid-west of Nepal. This region was the centre of most of the violence during the seven years of the Maoist Revolution in Nepal. Participants in this workshop shared horrific stories and more workshops have been requested in that region as well as Pokhara. Friends Peace Teams focuses on building long term relationships with peacemakers in difficult and challenging situations. Partnering with them provides the support structure for the ongoing AVP visits needed to reach sustainability in the Pokhara and Surkhet regions.

Afghanistan AVP was revised by Rosemary Epps, an Australian Quaker closely associated with AVP, who reported on the development of workshops there:

Violence has been the norm for so long in Afghanistan (more than thirty-five years and counting), that people wonder whether there could possibly be an alternative. In 2011 when Rosemary was working with Afghan colleagues involved in other peace and reconciliation initiatives or looking for a way to try to raise awareness of women's rights, the idea that AVP might help was raised. Although sceptical, her colleagues were very curious to find out more. The first full training of eleven facilitators was run in 2011 with Ann Ward. Later that year training was provided for eighteen mediators and legal advisors needing to help women involved in domestic conflicts.

In 2013, Rosemary returned to Afghanistan, together with Julei Korner, an experienced facilitator from Sydney, to fully train a group of twenty-three facilitators: teachers, religious scholars and community workers committed to raising awareness of women's rights in the provinces of Kunduz and Faryab. A further group of sixteen community workers from the Aga Khan Foundation also did a Basic workshop. Katherine Smith, from Sydney, organised manuals to be translated into Dari and the funding came from various sources through The Asia Foundation. It is hoped that forty-eight facilitators from another twelve provinces will be trained in 2014. It has been heartening to repeatedly receive this feedback from participants: 'We need these workshops to spread all over Afghanistan.'[16]

AVP International Gatherings
1990 New York, 2000 Oxford and 2002 Nigeria:

For most facilitators attending these gatherings, held every two or three years, it is an inspiring and energising experience. I have been lucky enough to have attended the last five of these.

Aoteoroa New Zealand, March 2004

This was the first International Gathering which I attended. We all – men and women – slept on mattresses on the floor of a Marai with enormous pillars representing ancestors around the walls. I felt very protected by these ancestors. This was the first time that I realised how our manuals were used all around the world. There seemed to be less variation in the way facilitators used or interpreted these compared with Christians' use of the Bible in different countries. I also experienced the value of the respect that AVP people show for each other. It diminished any feelings of shyness I had because everything anyone says is treated with respect. I met people connected with the beginnings of AVP – Steve Angell, Ellen Flanders and Elaine Dyer. Here we had just two men from Africa who were always dressed in suits. The two Gatherings after this one were predominantly African.

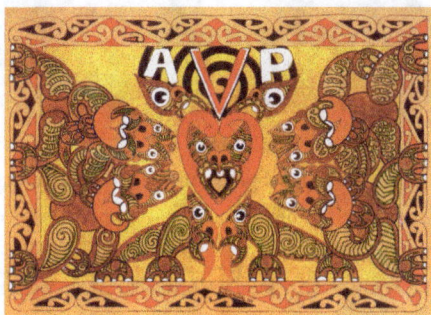

AVP Aotearoa postcard.
Photo: Sally Herzfeld

South Africa, August 2006

For this Gathering in South Africa 104 participants from twenty-three different countries gathered at Hartbeespoort Dam between Johannesburg and Pretoria. An essential part of this experience was that we shared the food, the culture, the languages, the history and the current concerns of our host nations. For five days we were all Africans.

AVP started in South Africa in 1995 and they have since developed programs in prisons, schools, universities, businesses, government bodies, NGOs, religious organisations and the community. There were facilitators from Burundi, Rwanda, Uganda, Kenya, Angola, Namibia, Sudan, Zimbabwe and the Congo. We learned that South African facilitators were responsible not only for spreading AVP in Africa, but also to Israel/Palestine, Hong Kong and China.

At that Gathering was where I first heard about AVP workshops centred on violence against women, post conflict reconstruction and prisoner rehabilitation. My main memories of that Gathering are of the young people who were present and being in a workshop with Steve Angell when he gave us hints on how to present our Transforming Power Mandala.

Young girls of the HIPP Club singing at the South Africa Gathering. Photo: Sally Herzfeld

The young people were a very active group who drummed, danced and sang at any spare moment. Their concert performance was very moving. They acted one of the typical AVP HIPP (Help Increase the Peace Project) club nights which they held monthly. Sitting in an informal circle they started by saying what had been happening in their lives. One girl was crying while she spoke about trouble within her family and how she wanted to leave home but didn't really know whether that was the best thing to do or not. They discussed this from all angles, offered sympathy and support, then had an energising game, before an AVP exercise and more singing, drumming and dancing.

At that Gathering discussions were held on the formation of an AVP International body. I also remember hearing about how four facilitators from USA and four from Uganda were sent by the African Great Lakes Initiative to train facilitators in

Rwanda in 2001. From then until 2006 they had done workshops in all provinces of Rwanda for community people, for gacaca judges, for demobilised soldiers and for released prisoners and victims. They trained people to better prepare them to facilitate restorative justice and reconciliation processes in their communities.

After the Gathering, I travelled to Port Elizabeth and co-facilitated three Basic workshops with teachers in the Nelson Mandela University. Hopefully, these teachers would then go on to do the Advanced and Training for Facilitators. A Conflict Management Team had been developed to help counteract the violence amongst students in the schools.

Kenya, September 2008

This was another very exciting experience. In Nairobi, I boarded at a Catholic convent from where I had assurance that it would be safe to walk to the Friends Meeting House. It was quite a large complex and there was a large number of African families there. They were dressed in dazzling white shirts or blouses and black pants or skirts. There were drums playing and lots of singing. Was I at the right place? Then I saw a small sign with an arrow leading to the room for the silent Meeting for Worship. This room was small, dark and very plain, but I felt a strong bonding spirit with the five or six of us who met, even though I didn't know any of them. Seeing the large, happy, chanting group was my first experience of 'Programmed Friends'. I was also surprised to see how many Friends' schools, churches and meeting places there were everywhere I travelled in Kenya. AVP workshops were very prolific and mainly linked with Friends. All were supported by AGLI. No matter in which group or country I participated in AVP, I noticed there is far greater similarity in the delivery of these workshops than in the manner of worship between programmed and non programmed Friends.

From Nairobi, I travelled by bus for about eight hours to a Friends Centre near Kakamega where I joined a team of local people to run a workshop with local people from rural communities. Several of these were teachers and I remember the role plays being mostly about men cheating on their wives or the land grabbing that happened during the post-electoral violence. The quality control of AVP was very strict at this place and I enjoyed the learning I picked up there. Before each workshop, participants wrote on a card something for which they couldn't forgive someone. At the end of the workshop, they were given back their cards and asked how they felt. I remember that all but one person said that they felt so light and good because they could now forgive. The one who still felt that he couldn't forgive told the story of how having his land

15

taken off him had caused so much hardship for him and his extended family. It was heart rending, but then he looked at the Mandala on the wall and said, 'If I follow that I will forgive and care for others, respect myself and expect the best.' Everyone clapped and there was a group hug.

Takatifu Gardens, a Quaker Centre where we stayed and ran the workshop near Kakamega.
Photo: Sally Herzfeld

At one of the first meetings at this International Gathering I was very moved by the fact that about 130 people from twenty different countries, could join together without practising and sing *Dona Nobis Pacem* in rounds – very uniting. Eleven African countries were able to be represented with the help of funding from the American Friends' Service Committee Dialogue and Exchange Program. The theme was 'The need to be self sufficient'.

After this International Gathering and back in Nairobi I joined a team with two locals and a Russian woman to facilitate a workshop in Roysambu, just outside the slum area. During the post-electoral violence, businesses and homes were burnt, people were hacked or burnt to death and many had to hide for several days. There were still thousands of people living in refugee camps because they had nowhere else to go.

In our workshops we have 'gatherings' in which everybody speaks on a certain topic. Amongst all the horrific stories that were shared with this group during the gathering on 'how violence has affected my life', there was one brilliant ray of hope.

Irene told of how she had gathered a group of fifty people together.

We wore white T shirts – some had PEACE written on them and our main aim was to stop 'ethnicity.' We marched and sang songs of peace preaching that together we are one. We are Kenyan – not separate tribes. As we marched around we said things like, 'I am a Kikuyu married to a Luo or a Kalenjin or the other way around. We have intermarried and our marriages are not going to be broken nor is our Christian background. We should love one another and live peacefully.' By the time we had finished we had more than 100 and we sang songs of peace.

We carried banners and papers about peace ... We were on TV. Police saw that we were peaceful and left us alone. I am not proud to be a Kikuyu, but I AM proud to be a KENYAN! There was no organisation – it just happened! We must bury our grudges and work together for the good of our whole country.'

Small discussion group with Innovative Irene in aqua T shirt.
Photo: Sally Herzfeld

After I had presented the session on Transforming Power at this workshop, participants were talking about ways in which they had used any of our strategies to resolve a conflict. One man pointed to each of the twelve guides and to all of the Mandala and could tell of ways in which Kofi Annan had used all of those to ease the tension and quell the violence in Kenya. I also realised that AVP and Quakers had played large parts in that peace making. I came home from that Gathering feeling very proud of being an AVPer and wanting to help with more and more peace making.

Guatemala, September 2011

A fortnight in Costa Rica before this gathering gave me an unforgettable experience in and around the San Carlos district of Costa Rica with Celina Garcia, Director of CEPPA (Centre for the studies/programs in Alternatives to Violence, a foundation in San Jose). She hosted about ten of us from different countries, who were doing Pre-Gathering workshops before going to Guatemala, and had two full weeks of activities planned. We joined in an entire city's celebration of the International Day of Peace on 21 September.

This city, with all its government and social workers and CEPPA had organised a full week of activities. We joined in the street parade of musicians, school children and many other local groups and ended up in a large hall. The highlight here was the performance of eight groups of international dancers and seeing groups from kindergarten children to senior citizens joining together to advocate Peace. We followed this with a workshop led by Dr Glen Martin on the topic of The Earth Constitution. This commenced with us introducing ourselves by saying, 'My name is … I am a human.' We didn't say to which country or religion we belonged.

Also during that week we AVP facilitators relished the opportunity to lead small workshops in a bilingual elementary school, then a high school, then with tertiary students. The accent on recycling in these institutions was very impressive. One example was that all the drink cartons were collected by a local women's group and somehow compacted sufficiently to be made into very strong desktops.

The second week saw us visiting a very poor slum community near the Costa Rican garbage dump. Here a wonderful person, formerly a Peace Corps worker, named Gail Nystrom, had begun with a Montessori school. From that she developed a project in the community of La Carpio and had attracted many volunteers. What we saw were two Montessori schools, two health clinics, an active mural painting project teaching nonviolence and safe sex with love, and newly painted 'houses'. We heard how this project dealt with finding employment opportunities for women and how they dealt with domestic violence situations.

As if that wasn't enough, we also visited an agricultural cooperative which was run by women who had been given a plot of land and were managing a very successful income-producing project. This upset some of the leadership of the men's group and the friction caused a lot of trouble in the community for twelve years. Over a four-month period, Celina had used her AVP type mediation skills to resolve this long-standing conflict.

Celina Garcia (front) with the women's group in Costa Rica.
Photo: Sally Herzfeld

Next came the amazing experience of joining a team of international facilitators to run a workshop in La Reforma, a Costa Rican prison. Some of the prisoners were from the Caribbean coastal area and were very lively performers at the end of the workshop – song, dance, drumming and laughing. It was hard to believe that they lived behind the razor wire in those corrugated iron buildings.

Presenting Transforming Power
and the Guides in La Reforma.
Photo: Sally Herzfeld

I could easily have stayed with Celina and joined in the work of CEPPA. This organisation is active in the protection and education of students against human trafficking and child prostitution, Celina even travels to Switzerland to conduct courses with selected young people.

However, I did fly to Guatemala and join with over one hundred participants from twenty-two countries in our International Gathering. We learned of the new Trauma Healing workshops that were being run in various needy places and there was a concerted attempt to develop cohesion between AVP groups within world regions. Various international committees were further developed. We now have an International Co-ordinating Committee to which the following committees report:

- Education Committee, which develops, translates and distributes manuals around the world. This also works on Best Practices.
- Finance Committee
- Information Committee
- Regional Committee which coordinates the AVP activities in the five regions
- Fundraising Oversight Working Group
- Information and communications
- International Gathering
- Legal
- Nominations

Ireland, July 2014

This was the most recent International Gathering. The whole group at the Ireland International Gathering. Photo : Blaze Nowara

This is the epistle forwarded to the rest of the world:

AVPI Gathering

Maynooth 13–19th July 2014

Epistle

Dear Friends

154 AVPers from 43 countries send greetings from the beautiful and historic surroundings of the Maynooth campus, Ireland. Under the guiding lights of diversity and inclusion we search in our different and similar ways for peaceful pathways into the future.

During this gathering of international faces and accents we made friends, shared stories, exchanged inspiring experiences and with an open eye focused on sustainability.

The size and emphases of this gathering, the largest in our history, left us in no doubt that our future is assured and will demand much of us.

The gathering not only brought people to one country, it did more than that, it connected various people to each other for the common purpose of the AVP and peace.

Our host country shared generously with us something of their work for violence against women, for homelessness, and of the long and ongoing process to reach peace in this land. We also listened with delight to the music of Ireland.

A thousand stories could be told but one must be shared, that of a visit to Wheatfield place of detention, where six inmate AVP facilitators shared their personal journeys:

- Though we may be in the gutters some of us still look at the stars.
- In the past the people were afraid to approach me because of my reputation of violence, since I became an AVP facilitator people find it easier to approach me when looking for help with their own problems.
- I came to prison … with a life sentence for murder … a year later I did my first AVP workshop … it taught me to turn my back on violence … it gave me the tools to change my life … it taught me a lot about empathy … which makes it less likely to be violent towards somebody. This is probably the most important thing AVP has taught me and if I can teach that to someone else I have done my job.
- it taught me to be creative … I write a lot of poetry now … I couldn't live without AVP … thanks AVP for making me the man I am today.

Finally one inmate concluded with the words of John O'Donoghue:
- May you realize that you are never alone, that your soul in its brightness and belonging connects you intimately with the rhythm of the universe.

This week we gained an insight into the AVP contribution in trauma work and the positive impact made against violence: we know that we need to expect the best. Finally we affirm the amazing job carried out by Irish and International AVPers which gave us a week and more of living, learning and loving together.
    Sabine, Odette & Yousif

Multicultural foursome (left to right): Trevor Clifton (Australia), Uysrih Awad Hamad Musa (Sudan), Maji PeterX (Nigeria), and James Bowes (Ireland). Photo: Sally Herzfeld

3. Developments in Australia

The Quaker Steve Angell brought AVP to Australia in 1990 at the request of Quakers Ron Smith and Lou Hunter in Queensland.

The beginnings of AVP in each state and territory

Perhaps research for this lecture may stimulate an interest in the history of the different AVP groups in Australia. I hope so. From the scarce material available, below is just an outline, a brief snapshot of the groups' beginnings, their evolution from Queensland in 1990 to the Northern Territory in 2006.

- With fellow American Ben Norris, Steve trained the first facilitators in Queensland in 1991. A couple of people from Melbourne also participated in this workshop.

- In 1992 Steve and Ben travelled to New South Wales to begin the training process there. Later Lou Hunter and Terry Pinnell, recently trained facilitators from Queensland, ran the Advanced and Training for Facilitators workshops. With more training led by Mark and Mary Hurst, Mennonites from the US Children's Response to Creative Conflict group, AVP (NSW) became self-supporting.

- In about the mid-1990s, Katherine Smith, Valerie Joy and other Quakers from Sydney plus local Quakers Ronis Chapman, Katherine Purnell and Charlotte Henderson, who had been to Sydney for training, ran a few community workshops in Canberra.

- David and Willie Walker, Quakers from Tasmania, benefited from a training workshop in Queensland, funded by the Quakers, and returned to their home state to deliver workshops in a prison there for many years.

- In 1994 Lou Hunter and Ray Horner from Brisbane went to Melbourne to help Quakers, Susannah and Ray Brindle to establish AVP in Victoria. Two non-Quaker women, Helen and Maria, were also involved.
- Elaine Dyer from New Zealand had been trained by Steve Angell. Together they helped Western Australia to train some facilitators in 1994 and to do its first workshop in Casuarina Prison in May 1995. Most of those early facilitators were Quakers, but not all.

WA's first workshop. Jo Vallentine WA, David Tehr WA, Stephen Angell USA, Elaine Dyer Aoteoroa, Ben Norris USA and Merrill Stokes WA, outside Casuarina Prison 1995.

- Jo Vallentine (Quaker) and Merril Stokes from Western Australia facilitated the first Basic workshop in South Australia in February 1996, with the group completing their Training workshop by the end of October. Facilitators from Victoria, New South Wales and the ACT were also involved in training the South Australian team.
- The first workshop held in Darwin, Northern Territory, was in 2006, one of twenty organised around Australia by AVP Interfaith and funded by the Australian Government's Department of Immigration. The AVP (Darwin) group was established in November 2007, after Basic and Advanced workshops were organised by Levin Diatschenko and Elizabeth Kwan (Quaker) from Darwin, and facilitated by Sabine Erika (Quaker) and Renate Kelaher from the AVP Blue Mountains group in New South Wales.[17] Ken Woods from Sydney helped develop the first group in Alice Springs.

The first National Gathering was held in 1994 when Steve, Ben and Elaine went to Sydney to provide Advanced Facilitators Training to AVP facilitators from Queensland, Victoria and Tasmania. There have been national gatherings for many of the subsequent years. These first gatherings were held in New South Wales and Victoria. The AVP Australia network of autonomous state and territory AVP groups was formed in 1998 and 1999. Since 2008 the National Gatherings have been held during the week immediately following the Australia Yearly Meeting week. The 2012 gathering in Perth and the 2014 gathering in Brisbane were also Asia West Pacific Regional Gatherings.

Developments by May 2014

AVP groups in Australia vary greatly in age, with the one in Queensland being the oldest and that of Darwin, the youngest. Some groups are incorporated and some are not. Some have gone into remission: currently South Australia and Canberra. Most groups keep in touch through the AVP Australia Network's monthly skype meeting. Through this network and the wider AVP facilitator email group, I invited groups to forward information about their beginnings, their developments and highlights up to May 2014. The information below comes primarily from their responses. Listed in reverse alphabetical order – just for a change! ☺

Western Australia

We have just held our twentieth anniversary and are amazed at how we have grown! Although we have about sixty facilitators only about twenty are active at present. Our main work has been in men's prisons. In Acacia we do fourteen workshops a year and hold three general meetings and training days with the inmate facilitators there. At Karnet and Wooroloo Prison Farms we do about six each year. Our inmate facilitators are the core of our success in these prisons. We have worked in the two women's prisons, but they ran out of rooms and time because of other compulsory programs. We are hoping to restart these workshops if we can train more facilitators who are free during the week.

At Warnbro Community High School, Olwyn Maddock has done an amazing job over the last six years. The AVP Youth Program is recognised as an endorsed subject and students gain one point for their WA Certificate of Education (Year 12) for each level they do. We have done a few in other high schools, but the ones I enjoy most are those we do in primary schools.

During the last couple of years we have done several with refugee groups through ASeTTS (Australian Services to Trauma and Torture Sufferers) or community workshops in which there are many mixed cultures. Basic workshops with young

Aboriginal people have been held with a young football team and with pre-employment groups. We are fortunate to have some 'dinky di' Aboriginal facilitators who are most important in these workshops. Some business or welfare groups have had us do workshops with staff or clients and I find these most worthwhile. Other ones we have done that I really enjoy are those with Muslim women. We have trained a few of them as facilitators and are looking forward to helping them run workshops in the Muslim schools.

We meet and have an office at the Perth Friends Meeting House, but try not to mention the Quaker influence in our workshops because we want to remain un-connected to any religious or political body. We say that we are a 'stand alone' organisation. We are an incorporated body, have tax deductable gift recipient status and are very fortunate to receive a donation from an anonymous trust fund each year. This enables us to travel to remote communities, do free workshops for disadvantaged groups or travel interstate to help other groups. We are also able to support with small amounts, other AVP groups within the Asia West Pacific Region and finance our facilitators to attend National and International Gatherings. This helps to keep us up to date with evolving ideas and trends.

With these funds, we were fortunate to be able to help develop and continue to support a group in the Kimberley region in our far North. Apart from money, to start a group, at least one passionate and dedicated person is needed to drive it. Jo Vallentine and Peter Fry did the first 'taster' session up there and were lucky enough to enthuse Astrid Gerrits who has been that driving force. Her workplace, Anglicare, has also been encouraging and helpful. Workshops have been held in the high school, with men's and women's prison groups, with general community groups, with staff members from welfare groups, and lately with remote Aboriginal communities. They have been able to expand to Derby prison and other Aboriginal groups outside the town. I am really grateful to have been able to take part in much of this development and relive my early years as a teacher with Aboriginal people.

Victoria

There were some workshops done in Loddon prison in the 1990s and AVP Victoria became incorporated in 1998.[18]

Over the two decades since its beginning, the Victorian group has always been a mix of Quakers and non-Quakers on the committee of management and the facilitators' panel. In fact, in the early years there was an equally strong Catholic involvement (they used to meet at the Sisters of Mercy retreat house). AVP was not an overtly 'Quaker initiative' in Victoria, though it is true to say that its survival has been underpinned by Quaker input (money, organising and attendees), and of course by Lou's devoted commitment and experience.

The Melbourne group has continued to run community workshops and this year has trained eight facilitators who are eager to be on facilitation teams. A workshop at the end of May included a number of young people from the Horn of Africa, and the idea is to introduce AVP to this community with the help of these participants. There has been inter-ethnic tension in the Melbourne suburb of Heidelberg and it is hoped that the Bayule Council might be interested in funding some workshops.[19]

By the time this booklet is being read, AVP Melbourne will have hosted the AVP National Gathering for 2015. Thank you, Victoria.

Tasmania

Willie and David Walker (Quakers at that time) ran workshops in Ulverstone and in Risdon Prison between 1993 and 1999. The group lapsed after a while but restarted after Rosemary Epps had become a facilitator in 2011.

This group has done a Basic workshop with a Quaker youth group in Hobart and another Basic plus one on Discernment for a Quaker residential weekend. They have done some 'taster' (introductory) sessions with Matriculation students at The Friends' School and given talks at their assembly. They have also done presentations to Women's International League for Peace and Freedom and Oxfam groups. One facilitator uses AVP ideas with immigrant teenagers in schools as part of her work for the Migrant Resource Centre. Another uses AVP spin offs as part of her work with staff and students at the Police Training Academy. It is hoped that a Basic workshop can be done with TAFE teachers in Launceston and at the Police Training Academy. In 2009 and 2010 workshops were held for the staff of the Tasmanian Polytechnic and in Launceston in 2011. Staff had been teaching a number of high-risk students, violent incidents had been common and staff morale was low prior to this. Many of the staff found AVP to be very helpful.[20]

South Australia

AVP SA was going strongly, but after 2005, it was 'unable to recruit enough facilitators who could commit to weekend workshops or to regular workshops in prisons during the week'.[21] Also, 'the work of continuing to offer workshops by the existing members had become too onerous'. At a public meeting on 23 June 2013, members agreed to dissolve the organisation.

From 1996 to 2006 AVP SA held 31 workshops: 20 Basics, 5 Advanced, 4 Training for Facilitators, 2 HIPP for Year 10 students. Approximately 240 people received training in nonviolence and 25 facilitators were trained. These facilitators gave a series of workshops in Alice Springs and helped other states when needed. In summary, many who attended the workshops said that they had a lasting effect and were 'helpful in all aspects of their life'.

Elizabeth Kwan (AVP Darwin) and I ran a Basic workshop for the Quakers of South Australia and Northern Territory Regional Meeting in Adelaide in October 2013 hoping that AVP SA might revive.

Queensland

An inspiring Regional Gathering was held in a beautiful tropical setting in January 2014. Here it was decided to create a book of Australian Transforming Power stories. Queensland is planning a set of workshops with refugees. In the Southern Queensland Correctional Centre between six and eight workshops are run per year. Community workshops are run as requested – not often. HIPP workshops are offered in some schools, mostly in the Redland Bay area near Brisbane. The active Management Committee meets monthly and has occasional catch-ups to which all are welcome. Their AGM is usually preceded by guest speakers and activities.[22]

Northern Territory

Less than three years after Darwin began in 2007, there was a small group of four local facilitators who continued to run community workshops with the help of more experienced facilitators from interstate. Then workshops beginning at Melaleuca Refugee Centre Torture Trauma Survivors Service of the NT in 2011 provided Darwin facilitators with more experience in facilitating, again with help from facilitators in NSW, WA and Qld. The Peace Leadership Training program, established by Justine Mickle at the Centre was funded by a NT government grant through the Department of Children and Families. It was renewed until mid-2014. By then, the program had trained twenty adult facilitators in several different ethnic communities (especially from parts of Africa) and seven youth facilitators at Sanderson High School. They are now gaining experience as apprentices in presenting workshops to members of ethnic communities. First Fridays, monthly training sessions for all those with an interest in practising their AVP skills, were introduced in February 2014 by Jordan Hoffmann, the Centre's Interim AVP coordinator. The formal end of the AVP program at Melaleuca has prompted much thought on other ways of continuing to offer AVP to refugees arriving in Darwin.[23]

Despite the transient nature of Darwin's population, also affecting our trained facilitators, AVP Darwin has held eighteen workshops in the general community and facilitated twenty-two refugee workshops. Other states have drawn on the Darwin experience of working with refugees. A new challenge is to respond to requests for workshops with Indigenous communities, and in the new prison in Darwin, while training enough local facilitators to make that possible.

Over the last few years several workshops have been held in Alice Springs, with Robyn Manley being the main driving force there. Again the transient population makes it difficult, but facilitators from Sydney and Perth travel to help.

New South Wales

AVP NSW started running workshops in 1992 in both prisons and the community. In 1994 they became incorporated and decided to concentrate on community workshops. They have averaged one a month since then. Initially many of the participants and facilitators were Quakers, but since then people from many faiths have been involved.

Graeme Stuart (Quaker) began community and youth workshops in Newcastle. The manual he used from the USA was *Help Increase the Peace Program* and since then our Australian workshops with young people have been called HIPP.

Over the years the AVP program has waxed and waned as in other states and territories, but there has been a very active program in five prisons where an average of 25 workshops were held each year. Quakers Laurel Thomas and Sabine Erika also ran workshops in the Blue Mountains community.

In 1997, Julei Korner and Lyn Doppler and their team of Special Education teachers developed an active AVP schools' program in the 40 inner city schools of the Port Jackson District. Over the next fifteen years, the team ran over one thousand youth or HIPP workshops in Sydney schools. They also visited Brisbane, Perth, Hobart, Darwin and Papua New Guinea, training locals to run HIPP workshops.

Highlights of AVP in NSW include:

- Support from Sydney Quakers over the last twenty years by providing the Devonshire Meeting House free of charge for the AVP First Friday support group which has held mini workshops on the first Friday of every month for over 14 years.

- In 2000, AVP facilitators wrote a course based on AVP for Technical and Further Education (TAFE) NSW. This was called Transforming Conflict. The course was then used nationally and in ten years, reached over one hundred thousand students
- 2003-2006 the training and support of facilitators who developed an AVP program in Papua New Guinea
- 2005 – 2006 ran a series of AVP Interfaith workshops in partnership with the Forum for Australian Islamic Relations (FAIR) This project of twenty workshops throughout Australia was funded by a grant from the Department of Immigration.
- 2008- 2012 trained and supported facilitators who developed an AVP program in Nepal.
- 2011- with AVP Tasmania did the same for facilitators who are developing a program in Afghanistan, then joined WA and Queensland to help develop a program in Darwin for refugees from Africa and Asia.
- AVP NSW facilitators have joined workshop teams in other states and overseas. Some have served on committees in AVP USA and AVP International and on the AVP board of trustees for both of these groups.
- AVP Sydney has written a number of local manuals and members have been on committees to update the manuals used worldwide. The *Sydney Concise Manual* was written to support refugee workshops. It is easy to translate and has been part of a collection of manuals that were distributed to all AVP country groups in the world.
- AVP Sydney is currently working in partnership with NSW Service for the Treatment and Rehabilitation of Torture and Trauma Survivors.[24] This program with refugees is called Community Conflict Transformation or Peace Leadership. Currently, monthly workshops are run and forty-three new facilitators with refugee background have been trained. This invigorated AVP group is now planning to double the number of workshops run per year with communities from different countries around the world.[25]

Australian Capital Territory

AVP started in 1995 with some Quaker facilitators Fionnan Brooke-Watson, Katherine Purnell and others, doing workshops mainly with Quaker groups. Charlotte Henderson worked in schools and liaised with a school counsellor who was training teachers. Some facilitators from Canberra did a number of workshops in NSW Parkville prison for youth offenders and helped Laurel Thomas establish AVP at the Junee prison. AVP ACT became less active by 2003 and was reactivated in 2009 when it started an AVP program in the new Canberra prison. This lasted until 2012 so AVP ACT is waiting to be revived again. Who will do it?

Coming full circle: Australians at the national and international levels

Australians had benefited from those bringing AVP to this country. They adopted the manuals developed and revised in the US for the three different courses, Basic, Advanced and Facilitator training. There was also a manual in 1993 (revised 1999) for the Help Increase the Peace Program (HIPP) for youth.

In the US the majority of workshops were in prisons rather than in communities and schools/youth groups. A different pattern emerged in Australian groups, where workshops in most states, were more often in communities rather than prisons

Adapting AVP to Australian circumstances

AVP NSW began developing its own set of manuals which led to the *AVP Sydney Concise Manual for AVP Youth, Help Increase the Peace, Peace Leadership: a concise manual for facilitators of Basic, Advanced and T4F workshops.* Most influential in this process was a small Sydney group, Julei Korner, in the Department of Education, Katherine Smith in TAFE and Malcolm Smith who coordinated AVP NSW. Katherine and Malcolm were honoured in 2008 with a Medal of the Order of Australia for 'service to the community through fostering peaceful conflict resolution and the promotion of interfaith understanding'.[26]

The purpose of the *Concise Manual* was to reduce the US manuals to a central core which could be easily understood by children, youth and new immigrants/refugees. Later, when they had mastered this core, they would be ready for the detail of the US manuals. Refugee participants in the Peace Leadership program at the Darwin's Melaleuca Refugee Centre found this manual more accessible than the US manuals, though even then preferred manuals translated into their own languages.

Influencing AVP in the US and around the World

Some Australians have developed leading roles not only in the AVP Australia Network but also in AVP International. John Michaelis, Katherine Smith and I, all Quakers, have had significant roles on committees of AVP International. Katherine and Elaine Dyer of Aotearoa/New Zealand were the non-US members of the four-member editorial team revising the *Facilitators Training Manual* for AVP(USA) and AVP International.[27]

4. What is an AVP workshop?

The best way to find out what an AVP workshop is like is to experience one. Because they are not always available in some parts of Australia – or of other countries, this is not always possible.

Imagine about fourteen adult participants, who have decided to attend an AVP Basic community workshop, gathering early on a Saturday morning. A team of three or four trained facilitators welcome and invite the participants to join them in a circle. This team has spent some hours beforehand, team building, discussing and preparing an itemised agenda, which provides the framework for the weekend. This can be changed and often is depending on how the participants respond. The first agenda goes up on the wall, together with the Philosophy, Themes and Guidelines posters and their messages are addressed during the first session.

You might also imagine that the participants are a group of inmates gathering in a prison, or a group of children in a primary or high school, or an ethnic group.

Elements of a Basic workshop

Materials

We are a grass roots organisation with simple basic materials that can be easily carried and are inexpensive. The light banners you see are made of polyester cotton with text written using permanent textas. For some cooperative-building team exercises we use newspaper or other recycled materials and we make good use of newsprint paper.

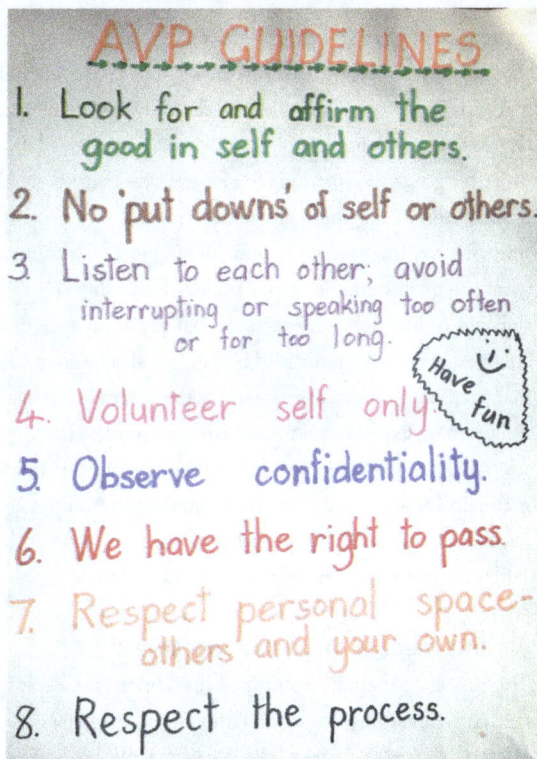

AVP GUIDELINES

1. Look for and affirm the good in self and others.

2. No 'put downs' of self or others.

3. Listen to each other; avoid interrupting or speaking too often or for too long.

4. Volunteer self only

Have fun :)

5. Observe confidentiality.

6. We have the right to pass.

7. Respect personal space— others' and your own.

8. Respect the process.

The AVP Guidelines.
Photo: Sally Herzfeld

Timing

Workshops usually take about eighteen to twenty two hours with ideally ten to sixteen participants and three or four facilitators. They usually run for two full days or three shorter days. Lately, we have been trialling variations to this with three consecutive Sundays or a Monday, Wednesday and Friday – whatever suits the group. The whole agenda consists of six to eight themes which build on each other so are often called Building Blocks.

Teamwork

All AVP workshops are conducted by teams of two to six trained facilitators, who have completed at least three progressive levels of workshops and gained experience as an apprentice. While one person is leading an exercise, the others can be looking after the logistics, observing and perceiving, and later responding to what is happening in a group. The team acts as a safety net and support, as members usually have different degrees of experience.

After giving instructions for an exercise there is no shame or embarrassment for a facilitator to ask the team mates, 'Have I left out anything?' Although we do, at times, have team leaders, the non-hierarchical, co-operative leadership modelled by the team is a great example of community leadership skills. It is thought that striving for stardom or hierarchical leadership can cause violence in one of its forms. In Western Australia we take it in turns to be the team leader for a day. This really means being the manager for team discussions and taking overall responsibility for that day. Of course, we also have experienced people who mentor the less experienced.

All team decisions are made by consensus, but guided by what's written in the manuals. These manuals were first compiled in America and contain all the information needed to run series of workshops. They are constantly evolving as facilitators try different ways of achieving a set purpose.

All volunteers; all teachers and learners

The posters of our Philosophy, Guidelines and Building Blocks indicate how we run our workshops. In prisons, the fact that we are all volunteers is very important. We all sit in a circle to make it easier to learn from each other. Many of us who are schoolteachers find this a challenge at first. We tend to want to stand up and TEACH rather than FACILITATE, which, to me, means 'make it easy' for the members to discover information for themselves.

Also important, from what participants say they appreciate, is that there are no lectures, no note taking, no powerpoint productions or tests. The workshop is very interactive. The fact that we can use almost the same agenda for all ages and types of group shows that through participating, the group sets its own level, and discussions develop about the special interests or needs of a group. Violence to a primary school child involves bossing, pushing in the canteen queue, cheating in tests; to a high school child and even in remote Aboriginal communities, it involves cyber bullying, swearing, vandalism, jealousy; amongst adults, whether they be community members or prisoners, substance abuse, revenge, anger and racism are common.

AVP Philosophy. Photo: Sally Herzfeld

Light and Livelies

These are like games or energisers which lift the spirits, cause plenty of laughing and usually have a hidden learning point as well. They certainly help with community building. They are placed in strategic places in all our agendas no matter what level.

Themes or Building Blocks

Before I did my first workshop I thought it would be all a matter of being given some strategies and then being annoyed or tested in various ways to see if I could control my animal instincts and respond peacefully. I was disappointed that role playing was only a small part at the end of the workshop. It wasn't until I had facilitated a couple of Basic workshops that I realised how important the Building Blocks were, to be able to resolve conflicts peacefully.

- **Affirmation** – We need a certain amount of self-esteem and confidence before we can
- **Communicate** effectively and contribute by
- **Co-operating** within a team. These skills used with respect for all and

- **Trust** in oneself and others make it possible to
- **Build community** and use
- **Transforming Power** to practise
- **Conflict Resolution.**

The themes as Building Blocks.
Photo: Sally Herzfeld

Early in the workshop we give ourselves a positive or aspirational name that starts with the same sound as our first name such as Super, Smiley or Sunny Sal, Caring Kelly, Generous Jim. The sessions of the workshop include gatherings in which every person speaks on a topic. At the beginning of the session on Communication the gathering could be: My positive name is … and I find it easiest to speak my mind when … This would be followed by exercises with small and large groups, discussions, light and livelies and role plays.

In the first session of a Basic there is an exercise called Affirmation in Twos and Fours. The participants are paired in some way and given one or two minutes each to tell their partners what they like to do in their spare time. Next they have the same amount of time to tell each other about their good points or their strengths. Many Australians have trouble with this one because they feel as though they are bragging. After this, each pair joins another so that there are groups of four and, in turn, each person introduces his/her partner to the others. During the processing which follows this exercise, participants say how affirming it was to hear someone tell others the positive things about them.

Transforming Power

Later in the Basic workshop we present the idea of Transforming Power. Transforming Power is the hub of AVP. Put simply, it is a power that can change a potentially violent situation to a peaceful one. We say that it is a power that is within each of us to use if we are open to it.

At times I toss up whether we use the concept as a noun or a verb. That is, we use a transforming power for transforming power.

It can be thought of as a resource. Steve Angell used five main strategies for solving conflicts peacefully and made them into a shape with the words Transforming Power in the middle. At the International Gathering in South Africa in 2006 Steve told the story about research done in a US university. The research listed the most common methods that were used to solve conflicts peacefully. It was a long list, which he and other facilitators condensed to make it more usable.

One night Steve was in his motel room trying to make some shape out of the five chosen strategies, a summary of all those methods. A friend dropped in to chat for a while and the next morning he asked Steve, 'How did you get on with your mandala last night?'

Steve said, 'My what?'

And his friend said, 'That thing you were making last night.'

Steve didn't show his ignorance at that point, but looked up a dictionary and decided that Mandala was an appropriate name for the collage he had made. We still call this our AVP Mandala. The two central elements are 'Respect for self' and 'Caring for others'. In a general way, these values seem to be the core of many different religions and cultures. They are very Quakerly! The outer circle contains the words 'Expect the best', 'Think before reacting' and 'Ask for a nonviolent solution'.

When thinking of any conflict which I have solved peacefully, I can see how each of those elements was used.

Mandala. Photo: Sally Herzfeld

During the session on this theme, we invite participants to share stories of times when they have solved a conflict peacefully or averted a possible conflict. After we have presented the Mandala in various ways, people can then see which parts of it they have used. We can then build on that experience and later explore how the Mandala can be used in many different situations.

Some Transforming Power stories given to me by prisoners for publication:

25th Birthday

I'd been with a girlfriend for more than three years. She was a nice girl and very pretty. We went out every week and I nearly always got into a fight with other guys. One night as we got into the car to go out she said, 'Sam, if you fight tonight, I will leave you!'

I said, 'Where's this coming from? You haven't said anything like this before!'

She said, 'Every time we go out and you fight it makes me feel that you're more interested in impressing other guys than impressing or being with me.'

It brought me up with a start! I said, 'But what will I do if someone asks for a fight?'

She said, 'Just hold my hand and walk away.'

I tried this and couldn't believe how big I felt! I felt much more of a man than if I had fought and won. I felt really strong! We stayed together for two and a half years after that and it made a big effect on me forever.

Sam

Dad's advice

I worked with a group which had contracts from state housing to remove damaged asbestos fences and replace them with other material. One day we were working on a fence with all the necessary safety gear and warning signs etc.

One guy from another house was just watching us all the time and complained that his fence wasn't being renewed. He was getting very angry and swearing. Next morning all his side fence was lying on the ground. He said it was the wind!! I knew there was no wind and told him so.

He said, 'Are you trying to tell me that I pushed the fence down by myself?' and he kept at it.

I was ready to have a go at him but my work partner said, 'Don't fight him. We have a contract to do just what we are told to do. Ignore him.'

I did this and just walked away.

Later I asked my Dad if I had done the right thing. He agreed and said, 'Most people who try to egg you on are just dickheads! Just think to yourself, I don't have to prove myself to them.'

This has been very helpful advice and my mates agree too.

Advanced

After completing the Basic, people are invited to take part in the Advanced level. The main difference between this and the Basic is that we discuss and do exercises on consensus and then the participants decide by consensus what theme they would like to cover for the remaining part of the workshop. Usual choices are between Anger, Stereotyping, Power/Powerlessness, Fear, Forgiveness, Communication, Relationships and that type of subject.

An exercise we do to illustrate consensus is called, Jelly Bean Guesstimate. A jar of jelly beans which has been pre-counted by a facilitator is passed around the circle so that each participant has three seconds to look at it. Each person then writes down how many he or she thinks are in the jar. They then get into pairs and try to come up with one number that both are happy with, then into fours and then eights and then the whole group. To come to a joint decision with which each member is happy, they are encouraged to respect and listen to each other's reasoning, not bargain or average the numbers. After the actual number is revealed there is a discussion on different types of decision making processes and the times when each of these is useful or harmful. The pros and cons and what is needed for consensus are listed before we attempt to decide on the theme that is going to be most useful or acceptable to all members of the group. I'm sure that many readers will see the links with Quakerism here.

In the last few years, new programs have been developed around Shame, Discernment, Trauma Healing/Awareness and we are working on Addiction.

At the end of an Advanced workshop, we give participants an opportunity to do some self-reflection. They either write a letter to themselves as a teenager (This is called 20/20 hindsight) or write their goals for the future.

20/20 hindsight stories

These were given to me by the inmate authors with permission to use in any of our newsletters or promotional material.

A letter to myself

If I had known then, what I know now. From the mistakes I've made and the wrong paths I have taken, and the advice I did not listen to, but I've learnt and am still learning from my mistakes so I thought I would write this letter of advice to me when I was 15:

> Look, Listen and Learn. Drugs will be an issue in your life and alcohol will lead you there. So, maybe a social drink every now and then, but the path of drugs will bring temporary enjoyment which will cost you more than the price you paid for it – financial – relationships – prison.
>
> **From Me to Me**

Dear Chris

I know you're probably sick of people telling you what to do, but I've got some mad ideas for you to get money, girls and success. Stick to your graff., just don't get caught up in the subculture and listen to this advice and you're gonna have a bright future.

You don't have to go to school, you can get your Yr 10 through TAFE and it's easy. Once you've done that you can get an apprenticeship. Try tiling. It's good money. Get a licence and a car and save some $$$.   Peace out!

Older you

Dear Adam

Life is full of adventure. Life is a continual learning experience. Learn to live like there is no tomorrow, but dream for the future. Don't let disbelief emotions control you. Life is too short to waste time on trivial issues. Don't harbour hatred or anger or resentment towards others. Learn to forgive because the only person who is hurt by blaming others is yourself.

Happiness is a journey not a destination. Don't think that if you get the car or that house or lots of money that you will be happy. Learn to be happy now. Learn to enjoy the good things in life such as family and friends. Enjoy the birds singing, the breeze blowing and the sun shining.

Be content with what you have. People are always chasing after the green grass on the other side, but once they get to the other side they realise that the OTHER side looks greener. People always want what they don't have. Learn to be content. Learn to let go. A man is defined not by what he has but by what he lets go.

Hey mate

I know you're only 15 but if you knew what I know now I think you would be so different. Just a couple of words of advice. I really want you to quit smoking. It just gets harder when you get older. Another thing – chill out, take it easy and try not to be so bloody angry. Oh, don't move back home. Some bad shit will happen if you do. Lay off the alcohol. It does you no favours and you don't need it.

On the 9th of July 2007 someone will pepper spray you and stab you after a party, so either don't go or go home in the first carload. Oh yeah, don't go to Northbridge after your work do. When you are looking for a taxi blokes try mobbing you and you end up smashing them all. I know it sounds pretty cool, but you end up in jail for four and a quarter years. Take it easy mate. THINK BEFORE YOU ACT.

Goals for the future story

My goal for the future is to start my own business, having my own workshop, building all types of different trailers, car carrying trailers, workman trailers, and even semi trailers such as flat top trailers, drop deck trailers and super lift tipper trailers.

I have worked in the fabrication field for many years, I am confident that I can do the work required as long as I can afford to buy all the machinery and equipment that is needed to do the work. There is also other work that may arise such as repairs and modification to existing trailers that I could also do.

If I don't achieve the goal I know I will become a successful law abiding citizen, of whom everyone will be proud. I would also hope to find a loving partner, and have a loving relationship and hopefully become a Dad before it is too late for me to do so.

From JB

Training for Facilitators

If people want to become facilitators they are invited to participate in a Training for Facilitators workshop where they experience team building, giving and receiving feedback and planning and presenting aspects of a Basic workshop. Self and team appraisal is also a big part of this training.

Following the workshop, if they want to continue, they have an interview with committee or experienced members of a group so that they know what their responsibilities would be as a facilitator and the group can judge whether that person would be a worthwhile facilitator or whether further training would be recommended.

5. Prison Workshops

Evaluation of prison programs

In America, most workshops are done in the prisons and some in schools. There is growing interest in the evaluation of prison workshops, both by prison authorities and facilitators. John Shuford, an American Quaker, circulated an *Evaluation on Prison Recidivism*[28] in 2013. Its chapter Description of evaluation outcomes and findings revealed:

> The Delaware recidivism study (Dr Marsha Miller and John A. Shuford) showed a reduction in overall recidivism of 46% over a comparison group of inmates for three years post release. More specifically, AVP graduates were convicted of another felony in those three years at a rate of only 13.5%. Compare this with the DOC [Department of Corrections] 2013 published recidivism rate for serious felonies (not all felonies) of 71%. Using these published statistics, AVP reduced recidivism for felony convictions by 80%.

In Australia, we have not yet done an official evaluation of our prison work, but each participant does a written evaluation at the end of each workshop and we gauge our effectiveness in a small way from this, plus the comments from prison staff.

Staff comments

One of the senior staff members of Acacia Prison was happy to collate staff comments in response to a request from AVP WA. We have been presenting workshops in that prison since 2002.

Hi Sally

Glad to give you some feedback:

We have been running the AVP program for numerous years here at Acacia. During those years we have literally seen hundreds of prisoners complete the voluntary programme from Basic, Advanced and T4F. I have seen numerous changes in people that have completed the different programmes – some that are obvious and some very subtle. The most obvious appear to be a sense of belonging to the group, empathy for others and a better outlook of the way they see things.

The prisoners who have become facilitators show diligence, empathy and an openness to help their fellow inmates.

The feedback we get from the prisoners is one of praise for the programme and that's why we love having you guys because anything that can help these guys break their recidivism cycle is good for us. I have kind of put it in a nutshell, Sally, I hope you don't mind.

Cheers

Elaine[29]

My experience in prison workshops has mostly been very positive. Prison staff are usually as supportive and friendly as their rules allow. Several in WA have seen so much positive change in the inmates that they have done the workshops themselves. Three have become facilitators but because of a conflict of interest they cannot facilitate within the prison.

Before entering the prison for the first time we read our guidelines about what we can or can't do or wear etc. We do not ask an inmate what his or her crime was. We just take them as we find them and try to affirm and build on the good that we see. All of these aspects of prison visiting are very important, but the one I have to repeat to myself before getting to the main gate is: 'Don't argue with the staff. Accept whatever rule they want to enforce without telling them that we didn't have to wear a belt for the duress alarm last time or that we've always been allowed to take in masking tape and so on.' Rules can be different every day and it's important for the continuing of AVP that we just keep that AVP purpose in our minds and comply happily.

Inmate participants

While the program for inmates is substantially the same as that offered in schools and communities, there are some differences. An important part of the AVP philosophy is that participants and facilitators are volunteers. This is particularly evident in prison workshops. Of course we get inmates who participate in AVP because they believe

44

it will look good on their parole application. Some of these are the cynical ones who argue with us, don't like the childish games, 'take the mickey' and are generally disruptive. Only once have I felt challenged by one who obviously held power over the others. If he gave a sign of approval – it was OK for others to participate. If he screwed up his nose and gave negative body language, then continuing in a way that can be beneficial for all was very difficult. Mostly I have found them to be very grateful and appreciative that outsiders can give up three days and spend them with the 'likes of us'. In an exercise where we divide into pairs in concentric circles and talk about various subjects, can you imagine what it feels like when a big tough guy talks so gently about something personal because 'You remind me of my Nan'?

A brainstorm on Violence/Nonviolence done early in the Basic reveals that there are many types of violence that don't involve physical fighting. We can usually come up with a simple definition of violence as being anything that hurts physically or mentally. This can include damage to things or country. When talking about the main causes of violence, I have noticed that a very large proportion of the prisoners say they wouldn't be there if it weren't for drugs and alcohol. We facilitators often come away wondering how on earth such nice men could be in prison.

They show deep remorse and shame for the ripple effect their misdeeds have had on their victims and their loved ones. The shame, embarrassment and hurt shows up during one topic that we speak about to another person – 'A person I respect and why'. So often for the men or women, it is their mum or grandmother – the ones who come and visit them and give support, no matter what.

During an exercise about empathy, we divide into small groups of four and write on a card, 'A challenge I am working on is …'. We complete that sentence, fold the card and put it on the floor between us, mix them up and then pick up one that isn't our own. In turn, we then read it as though it is our own and say how we are feeling about that challenge. A common one I pick up is about how to do enough programs to get parole, stay off the drugs and be a good dad to my kids. The feelings I express about this include feeling sad that I am missing birthdays and special events with my kids, frustration because there are not enough programs in this prison, but hopeful because the board is going to 'sit on me' very soon.

We used to write, 'A problem I am working on is …' but now we prefer to talk about challenges, and we used to say, 'It is making me feel …' but now we try to practise being in control of our feelings and not letting anything make us feel anything. Do you recognise some Quakerly self discipline there?

At the end of a workshop we do Hassle Lines and Role Plays to practise what we have learned. The facilitators try to choose scenarios to be acted in the Hassle Lines, so that they are relevant to the group. Sometimes they are too close to the bone for people to want to act. One day we tried, 'You came home from a night out with the boys and found another guy in bed with your missus.' No way would they act that, even though that sort of thing was the cause of some of them being in prison. It was relatively easy to calmly discuss what could be done, but while acting in that role, emotions could be aroused to danger levels or it wasn't the sort of incident that any of them wanted to relive.

Inmate Evaluation

Workshop evaluation forms are filled in before the presentation of certificates and from the comments made on these we can amend the program for the next similar workshop.

The following are some of the comments we receive:

- For these three days I felt like I wasn't in prison.
- I felt like I was an ordinary person.
- I've just realised that I haven't sworn for three days.
- I have never laughed so much in one day.
- It's the first day since I've been in prison that I haven't been scared of having my head kicked in.
- Coming to this course makes me realise that I really do have problems.
- The workshop created trust before approaching issues, it was non judgemental and esteem building. We were a group of humans, not inmates.
- There is a challenge implementing some of these tools on the inside versus the outside. Help people understand this and suggest ways. (They might try on the inside and just give up.)
- Run the workshop longer so you can review everything covered to get other perspectives to compare with your own.
- Make the Gathering questions aimed more at violence situations: for example, 'When was the last time you thought before you reacted? And why?' – focus on more realistic questions.
- I realised that my problems were minor compared with others.

- I used 'I' messages on the phone to my wife last night –AND IT WORKED!

Women prisoners:
- We learn a lot about ourself and others in a lot of ways and situations for positive outcomes.
- Learn about violence because when I go home I will be able to talk to others about it.
- Self respect and understanding different situations for a win-win solution.
- What I liked about the workshop is that I learnt about myself and that violence is not a way to solve issues. I learnt about listening to others and to be patient.
- The workshop was fun and learning more skills. It taught me more about seeing the rights and wrongs. It showed me to be a better person and what I will do in the future
- We did hard things. We did good things, helping and sharing.

Inmate facilitators

Many inmates become facilitators and are a great strength to AVP within the prison. They organise the workshops, enthuse others to participate and are great role models. Most prison workshops have at least two inmate facilitators who are on a team with at least two outmates. Having inmate facilitators gives the workshop more credibility. We get really excited when an ex-inmate facilitator rings us after release. He is then warmly welcomed into our community group and becomes a very valuable member of our workshop teams. One such person is Nick Vassallo who joined our community committee, has facilitated multicultural community workshops and done public speaking about AVP. He and his wife, Lyka, have become like family to us.

This is Nick's story[30]

My name is Nick. I am 42, married, I earn 200k a year, I am a manager for one of the largest construction companies in the Southern hemisphere. I am a high distinction student working my way through towards a PhD.

However, 10 years ago, I was lying in my prison cell in a maximum security prison, thinking to myself, '8 years to go'. I woke up each morning, wondering if I was going to make it through the day to see the next.

Life has not been rosy. Mum and Dad split up when I was 4. I started smoking weed when I was 12 and moved to methamphetamine at the age of 30. I was charged and found guilty of a rather violent crime which cost me 8 years of my life.

Prison is not what you see on TV. It is hell! I quite often remember thinking to myself, 'How could such a place exist in this modern world.' There was a lot of violence – someone getting stabbed each day. I kept my head down and tried to get through my sentence.

One day I was sitting at a table during our one-hour recreation time talking with a few guys. This chap by the name of Jack walked over and asked one of the guys if he was still available on Sunday to help with some cooking in the Visit Centre. This guy said, 'No!' I remember thinking to myself, 'What else could he possibly have planned?'. It's not like we have a busy schedule. Anyway, I offered to help Jack out. I thought it might kill some time in my day.

On the day I got talking to Jack, he was telling me about himself. He had a PhD and was thinking about doing another one. He was serving a life sentence and went on to tell me about this organisation called AVP. I was intrigued. He went on to say that there was cake and biscuits. I was even more interested as cake and biscuits are very rare in prison. He mentioned that there was a workshop coming up and I was welcome to attend.

A couple of weeks later, totally allured by the prospect of free biscuits and cake, I attended this AVP workshop. I looked around. There were about 16 other prisoners. In walked these two little old ladies with a suitcase. I had a chuckle to myself and thought, 'What would these little old ladies know about violence?' One thing I did notice was the respect they received from Jack and another inmate facilitator, Fred, who I had also got to know and respect.

I completed the three-day workshop. The feeling for me was somewhat overwhelming. It was like waking up on the morning and looking at the ceiling and seeing a huge sign saying, 'Next week's lotto numbers are …' I felt as if I had direction. I learnt a vocabulary of new words that I didn't know existed. I had made 16 new friends with a common goal, but most of all I knew and understood that conflict can be resolved without the use of violence and there can be a win/win situation for everyone. I learnt about affirmation, empathy, communication, team building and having respect for myself and others. I went on to do my Advanced workshop and then the Training for Facilitators.

A few months passed. Two guys walked into my cell. They demanded my medication. I was on pain medication for a serious back injury. I was a target in the prison system for any junky wanting his next fix. I, of course said, 'No' and explained that I needed the medication. This didn't matter to them. They wanted it! They pulled out a couple of 'shives' [homemade knife made for stabbing someone]. I knew I was in trouble but tried to remain calm and negotiate. It was no good. I copped a whack to the jaw and I lost my medication. I felt powerless.

Funny thing was, a few weeks later I was getting ready to facilitate an AVP workshop and in came one of the gents who had pulled a knife on me. I notified the other facilitators that this was one of the guys who had attacked me previously. I was asked if I wanted him removed from the program. I thought about it, but said, 'No! If anyone needs this workshop it's this guy.' I felt as if my power had been restored. I didn't say too much to the gent and he was also keeping to himself. During lunch I walked up to him with confidence restored and asked, 'How are you enjoying the workshop Dave?'

He looked down at the ground for a while then made eye contact and said, 'Nick, I'm really sorry about what happened. I was desperate. I'm really sorry.'

I said, 'Let's forget about it. I'm glad you're in the workshop.' This gave me a great feeling to be able to forgive.

Dave became a good friend. He and his friends became my protectors, and no one ever attempted to take my medication again. I admired his strength and willingness to make a change. He kicked his drug habit and got healthy.

What has AVP done for me? It has given me direction in life. It has helped me set and achieve goals. It has taught me to focus. It has given me skills to communicate and see things from the other side of the fence. It has helped me resolve conflicts at work so efficiently that I have worked my way up into a management position. It has helped me with relationship issues. It has given me a positive outlook on life. Best of all, it has given me confidence. It has given me a sense of community and, best of all, it has given me family. Thank you!

6. Youth programs

Katherine Smith of AVP (NSW), on her return from the US National Gathering in May 2013, reported a key conversation Dr Lafeyette had with Dr Martin Luther King in Memphis, when he gave the Mountain Top Speech on 3 April 1968. Katherine said:

The next morning, Dr King said to Dr Lafayette, 'The next project for us will be to take this non violence training to schools.' He then left the office and was assassinated that afternoon.

Dr Lafeyette then turned to me, his eyes moist, and looking at the Australian AVP Youth Manual said, 'We have not been able to do this, but you from Australia have put Dr King's dream of non violence in schools into practice.'[31]

A South African example

There are youth programs functioning in schools in other countries, but as I got to know Stan Jarvis at International Gatherings I have kept in touch with him and the work he does from the Quaker Peace Centre in Cape Town. Below is a summary of a report of Stan's work:[32]

They started in 2010 by training some teachers who have delivered mainly AVP Basic workshops to various high schools and to peace clubs. In 2013 they did some workshops in primary schools. Because of the passion for AVP three teachers from three different high schools have been responsible for enthusing other teachers and implementing AVP in Maitland High School, St Andrews High School and Oude Molen Technical High School. They have developed a model of training Grade 10 and 11 pupils as peer facilitators and them training Grade 8 – 10 pupils in return. Facilitators from the QPC will support these schools until they can anchor the program therein and ensure sustainability.

The highlights for the QPC have been the fact that young facilitators have been willing to give up weekends to train pupils in other schools. Another instance was when a group of participants at one school initiated a fundraising campaign to improve facilities at their school.

Western Australian examples

Our ground-breaking program in Western Australia, which I mentioned in chapter 3, was initiated by the school psychologist and the school chaplain. Workshops were done with peer leaders until they became facilitators who then helped run workshops for other students. Warnbro Community High School has a mixture of cultures – Aboriginal, Maori and others. Sometimes Olwyn has run mixed groups and sometimes has separated the ethnic groups. She has usually found that taking the group away from the school surroundings to another building or for an overnight camp works very well. Because the AVP Youth Program there is an endorsed program for years 11 and 12, the participants keep a journal during the workshop. Apart from this, the agenda is much the same as for any community group.

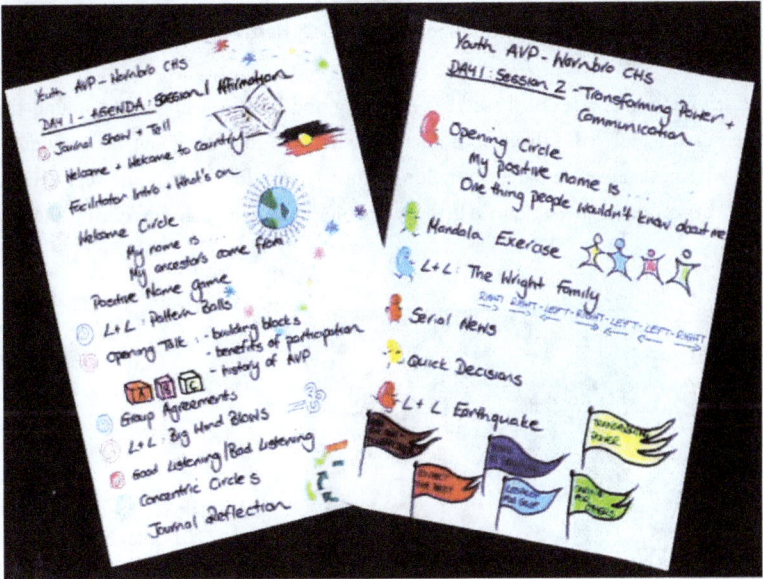

Bright and cheerful agendas for a high school youth program.
Photo: Sally Herzfeld.

For the pre-employment Aboriginal youths we have adapted the agenda to include discussions or exercises such as 'the qualities that an employer looks for' or the importance of being able to speak confidently.

The most obvious result our workshops have achieved with special classes in the Kimberley has been the increase in confidence and the group bonding that developed.

In primary schools we call the program HIPP or Help Increase the Peace Project. We change the names of things but the program has the same elements as an adult program.

What's On = Agenda

HIPP chain = Gathering

Help Hipp Happen = Guidelines

Instead of the Mandala we have a set of keys showing the various strategies.

The HIPP keys used in Western Australia for primary school workshops. Photo: Sally Herzfeld

Each child gets a set of these keys on a ring and has fun using them around the playground. I received a thrill from a parent when she told me about her very quiet child who never tells his parents anything about school. He came home very excited about the keys and was able to tell them how he had used each one during the last two days.

Year 6 Helena College students, August 2014, play 'We've fixed our broken squares'. This is a team building exercise about being aware of the needs of others. Photo: Sally Herzfeld

7. Community programs

Community workshops are held after advertising generally or with particular groups that have approached us. In WA we have done a series and trained facilitators from the staff of a women's refuge. At a Salvo's Hostel in Darwin, there was a mixture of staff and clients. This works well.

General community

A wonderful workshop which was advertised in the general community involved four local people from a hills village near Perth and four women from Iran and Afghanistan. One member of the facilitation team was Trevor, an Aboriginal who brought his guitar and didgeridoo. At lunchtime on the first day he played his didge, and another man played the clapping sticks while I led all the women (hijabs and all) in an Aboriginal women's emu dance. Next, Trevor played his guitar and sang while the others danced to the rhythm. The next day, the refugee women brought a cooked meal for us all and made us sit down all together and eat with knives and forks. Although understanding English was a problem, the bonding in the group was amazing. As one of the locals left she said, 'Thank you for the weekend. It was [sob, sob, sniffle, sniffle] overwhelming.'

Written evaluations from participants in community workshops include:
- I have learned to acknowledge and work through my underlying anger and to recognise my fears. To ask for help to resolve issues if I need to.
- I enjoyed the whole workshop. The facilitators were great and I'm awestruck that they do this on a voluntary basis. I'll use the information learnt in everyday life.
- I gained greater determination to eliminate violence from my life.

Some states have done interfaith workshops with success. In Perth the series we did with Muslim women involved some very deep and sincere discussions. They showed a great ability to empathise. To our Guidelines, some people add, 'Be culturally sensitive.' One of the Muslim women helped me relax in their company because she said, 'It is up to US to speak up and let you know if anything is done or said that could be offensive to our religious beliefs.' Lovely!

Construction – A team exercise completed by a group from a community workshop near Perth, June 2014. Photo: Sally Herzfeld

Aboriginal workshops

Henry Reynolds, a highly respected Australian historian who has widely researched and written about Indigenous and European relations in Australia, acknowledged the work of a visiting British Quaker. In his book, *Forgotten War*, Reynolds recognised that 'between the 1830s and 1840s ... James Backhouse was a great supporter of Australian Aborigines and was an advocate for land rights'. Backhouse had arrived in Hobart in February 1832 and left Australia from Fremantle in February 1838. Although spending most of his time in Van Diemen's Land [later, Tasmania], he had gone as far North as Moreton Bay and along the south coast with short stays in Melbourne, Adelaide, Albany and Fremantle.[33] I think James Backhouse would be pleased with the work AVP is now doing with our Aboriginal people.

In WA, we have been asked to go to remote communities to help reduce the violence that is unfortunately happening there at Beagle Bay, Balgo, Noonkenbah, Wangkatjungka, YiYili, Yakanarra and One Arm Point. For cultural reasons, these workshops are usually done in separate gender groups. The desire and longing for a peaceful existence is so strong, but the cultural requirement for 'Pay Back' makes this difficult. Tribal feuding also happens, mostly because people have been shifted from their own country to live with another group. One person told me that it's the fight for land rights which has split communities and families. How can this be addressed in AVP workshops?

Mowanjum children doing the Virus Communication Exercise. Photo: Sally Herzfeld

I have had some fun with language differences in remote Aboriginal community workshops.

One of our guidelines is 'We have the right to pass.'

One woman said, 'What do you mean? We know it's all right to die, but we don't expect to be doing it here!'

A Light and Lively we play involves throwing kush balls around in a set pattern so it is called 'Pattern Balls'. I'll leave you to work out why one young man was not going to play that game!

Back to back drawing at a community workshop in Derby, WA. Photo: Sally Herzfeld

Written evaluations from groups include statements like these:

- I liked learning about what people are doing in our community and also how to be strong against violence and mainly I liked coming together and getting strong women together to share stories and help them be more strong.
- Violence hurts community.
- I learnt to respect myself and others.

Refugee groups

AVP workshops are organised for special refugee groups in Darwin, Perth, Sydney and Brisbane.

In Perth it is called Peace Leadership and has been organised through ASeTTS (Association for Services to Trauma and Torture Sufferers). Some facilitators who have been trained in these groups hope to run workshops within their communities.

Peace Leadership in Queensland is organised in conjunction with the Multicultural Development Association.

Peace Leadership in Darwin is managed by the Melaleuca Refugee Centre Torture Trauma Survivors Service of the NT.

In Sydney, it is called Community Conflict Transformation and is supported by Service for the Treatment and Rehabilitation of Torture and Trauma Survivors (STARRTS).

8. What can you do?

For me, my involvement with AVP is a large part of my Quakerism. I try to make my life one of Faith in Action. Weekend workshops and quality time with family is higher on my priority list than attending Quaker Meeting, but in my morning meditation time I feel very connected to the spiritualism of the Society of Friends and people I know who are trying to make a difference.

'You must be the change you want to see in the world,' said Gandhi.
I became interested in AVP after hearing that the Perth group had headquarters at our Meeting House. Jo Vallentine seemed to be the organiser and because Dad had been with Jo on various protests I knew enough about her to want to join with her in this project. I did the three levels of training in a men's prison in 2002/3 and have been facilitating with many different groups within and outside Australia ever since.

While dealing with family and people in the other organisations to which I belong, I appreciate the constant reminder of conflict resolution or avoidance strategies that I receive during workshops.

I also gain great satisfaction from witnessing the results of AVP, including the written evaluations at the end of the workshop and the reports of the changes it has made in people's lives. Can you imagine the thrill if you are out somewhere and a smart young man calls out, 'Hello Smiley Sal'? That well dressed, confident looking young man was an ex-inmate.

The experiential and personal nature of workshops fits in very well with teaching methods I used with all my students during my career. I always tried to make lessons relevant by starting with something practical and of interest to those particular children.

If you feel that AVP could be a part of your life you could:

become a facilitator, if you

- can make time during the week or on weekends (young retirees, self-employed, students)
- wish to understand yourself and others more fully, to experience the joys and fun of living in peaceful communities
- can be a peace-loving role model who enjoys working with people. This is a necessary qualification also!!
- are free to travel. This would mean that you could help in remote communities or other countries.

join a committee.

Maybe facilitating is not for you, but you could help the cause by being a committee member.

We need

- secretaries
- IT specialists who could keep a database of participants and facilitators or look after a website
- treasurers, to look after the accounts and apply for grants
- marketers with desktop publishing skills
- someone with contacts to groups who are likely to request a workshop
- someone to arrange for the workshops, organise them and keep our kits replenished on time
- donors of tax deductible gifts.

The AVP website lists contacts for all Australian states and territories: www.avp.org.au

The closing done after a community workshop – Hands in for something good about the day.
Photo: Sally Herzfeld

Appendix

The following is a condensed time line showing when AVP was introduced to different countries. This information was taken from Fred Feucht's *My AVP Memories* and from information I received verbally and from country reports at the International Gathering in Ireland 2014. It is still evolving.

Between 1975 and 1988 AVP spread rapidly in the United States of America. Everywhere Steve Angell went he trained more facilitators who then helped take it to other areas and countries.

1989   Hawaii and Canada.
1990   Three visits by others started AVP in Alaska and the first International Conference was held near New York.
1991   Steve visited 28 states and 16 countries: including El Salvador, Guatemala, Costa Rica, Honduras, England, New Zealand and Australia.
1992   Steve with Elaine Dyer and Robert Martin visited New Zealand again, then went on to Brisbane and Sydney. A team went to Israel.
1993   Steve continued working around USA while others started AVP groups in Russia, Germany and Croatia.
1994   Workshops were run in Mexico, Nicaragua & Moscow.
1995   Steve and team to South Africa and Uganda.
1996   Hungary and under a Banyan tree near Bhopal in India.
1997   Maharashtra state in India.
1999   A group of Quakers from USA, Canada and South Africa toured Kenya, Burundi, Uganda, Rwanda and Tanzania.
2000   More done in Croatia and then Serbia.
2001   Friends Peace Teams (FPT) was formed and went to Rwanda, the beginning of the African Great Lakes Initiative (AGLI).
2002   then Burundi.
2003   then Kenya.
2004   Quakers took AVP to the Ukraine. Friends Peace Teams was formed in Indonesia.
2005   FPT to the east Congo.
2006   2007 a team went to Palestine and Israel
2007   2008 Korea started, an Australian team went to Nepal and FPT to Tanzania
2011   an Australian (with others) went to Afghanistan
2013   AGLI sponsored a workshop in the Kakuma Friends Church at a Refugee camp in north-west Kenya
2014   Kiev in Ukraine.

Endnotes

1   *Quaker Faith & Practice: The book of Christian discipline of the Yearly Meeting of the Religious Society of Friends (Quakers) in Britain (QF&P),* The Yearly Meeting of the Religious Society of Friends (Quakers) in Britain, London, 2nd edn, 1999, Ch. 24, Our Peace Testimony, Introduction.

2   *Quaker Faith & Practice,* 23.98

3   *This We Can Say: Australian Quaker life, faith and thought,* Australia Yearly Meeting of the Religious Society of Friends (Quakers), Armadale North, Vic., 2003, 3.96.

4   Interview of Steve Angell, All in One Films, Canadian Broadcasting Corporation.

5   Children's Creative Response to Conflict Program http://crc-global.org

6   Caroline Webster, *A Gandhian Quaker, Convict & Peace Teacher* 2012 p249 - 253,

7   Marilyn Stone, *Poughkeepsie Journal,* 28 Dec. 1977.

8   http://avpusa.hostasaurus.com/annual13.html

9   Extract from an interview between Bernard LaFayette and E.Ethen

10   avpinternational.org

11   Fred Feucht, *My AVP Memories,* Feucht to Author July 2014. See also the appendix

12   http://www.quakersintheworld.org/quakers-in-action/204 21 July 2014

13   David Zarembka, African Great Lakes Initiative, *Peaceways,* Spring-Summer 2014, p.3

14   Val Liveoak, Peacebuilding en las Americas, *Peaceways,* Spring-Summer 2014, p.6

15   Asia West Pasific Initiative, *Peaceways,* Spring-Summer 2014, p.10

16   Report written by Rosemary in May '14

17   Elizabeth Kwan, Coordinator, AVP (Darwin), 27 July 2014

18   Ray Brindle (Quaker) to author 23 May 2014

19   Bev Polzin(Quaker) to the author 22 & 23 May 2014

20   Rosemary Epps & Katherine Smith (Quakers) to author July & August 2014

21   AVP SA – A Report of Activities 1996 – 2013 by Jo Jordan (formerly Juchniewicz), 29 June 2013

22   Richard Denning to author June 2014

23   Elizabeth Kwan, coordinator AVP Darwin 2014: Alternatives to Violence Program: 'Peace Leadership Training': Report to NT Dept of Children and Families, Darwin, Community Development Dept, Melaleuca Refugee Centre 2014

24   (STARTTS – www.startts.org.au

25   Katherine Smith AVP NSW August 2014

26   www.itsanhonour.gov.au

27   Alternatives to Violence Project, *Facilitators Training Manual with Continuing Learning Material,* (1992), St Paul, Minnesota, AVP(USA), revd edn 2013.

28   John Shuford Crimesolutions.gov Application Description.pdf

29   Elaine Toovey, Resettlement Office, Acacia Prison, May 2014

30   Nick Vassallo to author April 2014

31   Katherine Smith to author, Regional Gathering, Springbrook, Queensland, Australia. Jan. 2014

32   Stan Jarvis to author, April 2014

33   Henry Reynolds *A Forgotten War* Sydney, New South Publications, 2013

Bibliography

Note: the information in this book is as correct as I could make it from information received verbally, written and by research. I would like to think it is an evolving document and welcome corrections, amendments and ongoing information. sallyherzfeld@ozemail.com.au

Published sources

Apsey, Lawrence S and Eppler, Karen *Transforming Power for Peace*, AVP project and Quaker Press of FGC

AVP Australia www.avpaustralia.org

AVP Australia News www.avpaustralia.org

AVP Manuals published by AVP/USA, Inc avp@avpusa.org

AVP/HIPP Sydney Facilitators Training Manual, c AVP(NSW) www.avp.org.au

Canadian Broadcasting Corporation *Steve Angell* www.allinonefilms.com/html_pages/angel.html 1991

Children's Creative Response to Conflict Program http://crc-global.org 'this we can say' *Australian Quaker life, faith and thought*, Australia Yearly Meeting of the Religious Society of Friends (Quakers), Armadale North, Vic., 2003

Garver, Newton and Reiten, Eric *Nonviolence and Community Reflections* on the Alternatives to Violence Project, Pendle Hill Pamphlet 322

Melaleuca Refugee Centre (2014) *Alternatives to Violence Program: Peace Leadership Training report to NT Department of Children and Families*

Peaceways Spring Summer 2014 Friends Peace Teams publication

Projects worldwide www.avpinternational.org/worldwide

Quaker Faith and Practice: The book of Christian discipline of the Yearly Meeting of the Religious Society of Friends (Quakers) in Britain (QF&P). Yearly Meeting of the Religious Society of Friends (Quakers) in Britain, London, 2nd edition, 1999

Reports from Kenya: www.agliftpt.org/rfk

Reynolds, Henry *Forgotten War* Sydney, New South Publications, 2013

Shuford, John 2013 pdf Crimesolutions.gov Application Description *Evaluation of Prison Recidivism*

Stone, Marilyn, *Poughkeepsie Journal* 28 Dec. 1977

Taplow, Alan *Alternatives to Violence Project of Vermont* ataplow@vtlink.net

Umino, Kaori (1983) *Alternatives to Violence Project: A Quaker Approach to Rehabilitation*

Webster, Caroline *A Gandhian Quaker, Convict and Peace Teacher,* Creative response to Conflict, US 01 January 2012

www.quakersintheworld.org/quakers-in-action 21 July 2014

http://avpusa.hostasaurus.com/annual13.html

http://en.wikipedia.org/wiki/Bernard_Lafayette

Unpublished sources

Fred Feucht *My AVP Memories* to author 21 July 2014
John Michaelis, Reports on Nepal and Friends Peace Teams
Katherine and Malcolm Smith, AVP NSW
Nick Vassallo talking to author, February 2014
Notes taken by the author during lectures and workshops at AVP International and
    National Gatherings
Reports from Australian groups for Skype meetings of the Australian network
Stan Jarvis, Report on Youth programs in South Africa

After reading this, many more Friends might well want to be part of this inspiring work.

THE JAMES BACKHOUSE LECTURES

2001   *Reconciling Opposites: Reflections on Peacemaking in South Africa*, Hendrik W van der Merwe

2002   *To Do Justly, and to Love Mercy: Learning from Quaker Service*, Mark Deasey

2003   *Respecting the Rights of Children and Young People: A New Perspective on Quaker Faith and Practice*, Helen Bayes

2004   *Growing Fruitful Friendship: A Garden Walk*, Ute Caspers

2005   *Peace is a Struggle*, David Johnson

2006   *One Heart and a Wrong Spirit: The Religious Society of Friends and Colonial Racism*, Polly O Walker

2007   *Support for Our True Selves: Nurturing the Space Where Leadings Flow*, Jenny Spinks

2008   *Faith, Hope and Doubt in Times of Uncertainty: Combining the Realms of Scientific and Spiritual Inquiry*, George Ellis

2009   *The Quaking Meeting: Transforming Our Selves, Our Meetings and the More-than-human World*, Helen Gould

2010   *Finding our voice: Our truth, community and journey as Australian Young Friends*, Australian Young Friends

2011   *A demanding and uncertain adventure: Exploration of a concern for Earth restoration and how we must live to pass on to our children*, Rosemary Morrow

2012   *From the inside out: Observations on Quaker work at the United Nations*, David Atwood

2013   *A Quaker astonomer reflects: Can a scientist also be religious?* Jocelyn Bell Burnell

2014   *'Our life is love, and peace, and tenderness': Bringing children into the centre of Quaker life and worship*, Tracy Bourne

www.ingramcontent.com/pod-product-compliance
Lightning Source LLC
LaVergne TN
LVHW022325080426
835508LV00013BA/1332